CAPTIVE

Captive

A Collection of Poems

LINDSAY GORDON

Lines By Linds

Copyright © 2024 by Lindsay Gordon

All rights reserved. No part of this book may be reproduced in any manner whatsoever without written permission except in the case of brief quotations embodied in critical articles and reviews.

First Printing, 2024

To Lex and Rocket —
for showing me unconditional love through my battles with Pain, and for being the sweetest reminders of Freedom I have ever known. I love you endlessly.

To my family and friends —
for displaying such empathy and understanding through it all, and for being safe spaces for me to not always have to put on a brave face. I thank God for you constantly.

PREFACE

Sometimes the sweetest surprises come out of the darkest times. I wasn't planning on writing a book when I started putting pen to paper, but rather to jot down a few lines that came to mind while a severe chronic migraine kept me from sleeping yet again. Even though I have loved reading and writing my entire life, I still had never really pictured myself writing a book. But once the idea of personifying Pain and Freedom (and eventually also Shame and Despair) came to my mind within the context of a prison metaphor, I could not stop writing.

My journey with chronic migraine is far from over, but creating these poems has been incredibly therapeutic. There is something powerful about giving an abstract concept a name. It has given me some clarity in regards to what I am fighting against, and what I am fighting for.

My hope for this book is that anyone who struggles with chronic pain of any kind will feel seen, understood, and validated. Further than that, my hope is also that those who have never experienced chronic pain will become more understanding and empathetic towards those who suffer from it. Chronic pain can often be invisible – I know that it certainly can be with chronic migraine – so my hope is that this book will shed light on the very real, often lifelong battle that is chronic pain.

    Thank you so much for joining me on this journey, and for allowing me the opportunity to be honest and vulnerable with you. It means the world to me.

REMANDED

Here we go
again.
Pain found me
even though I tried
with everything I had
to hide in the
comfort of
Freedom.
No matter
what I do,
he forces his
way back
into my
life, at the
worst
times.

Pain turns me
around and
slaps
cuffs on my
wrists
before I can
put up a
fight.
Dazed, I
whisper in
disbelief,
What did
I do
wrong?
He growls back,
You dared
to take
up
space.

-Arrest

After Pain
throws me into
my cell,
his two favorite
guards,
Shame and
Despair,
begin their
torture –
they bang on the
bars,
mock my
cries, and
taunt me with
Freedom's
name.

I am in a
prison cell
fashioned by
Pain
in the most
insidious way.
He has
created
the one place
I truly
cannot escape –
my own body.

I'm tired of
somehow
always ending up
back here,

but it
doesn't
surprise me
anymore.

It stormed my
first night in
prison.
Each thunderclap
was a
punch in the
head from
Pain himself.

You would
think
that my
past sentences
would have
prepared me
for the
next one.

It never
actually gets
easier.

Pain has
stalked me
all my life.
He started
making his
presence known
slowly,
until he
became a
school bully.
Even when I
tattled on him,
Pain still
attacked me
indiscriminately.

Pain
eventually grew up
to become a
criminal.
The older I
got, the more
violent
his attacks
became.
Pain has stolen
so much from
me, and he
refuses to
return
what he

took.
I long for
the day
that Pain is put
behind bars instead.

Pain is a thief
who gloats.
He is not a
cat burglar –
he does not
care to
be stealthy.
Pain wants
all the
credit,
without giving
a reason
for
robbing you.
He just wants
you to
know

it was him.

Pain
has no
reason
to rob
people of their
health, joy, and
peace.
He does it
because he
can.

But I
wonder,
who robbed
Pain
first?

Pain used to
lurk in the
background
while Freedom
and I
played,
always keeping
me
in his sights.
He would
lash out
and
strike,
attacking more and more
each
year.
Time only made Pain
more and more
vicious.
The boy who used to
push me on the
playground
grew up to
become a
violent
sociopath.

My body is the
snitch
who alerted
Pain to my
whereabouts.

From the
moment
I caught Pain's eye,
he has pursued me
relentlessly.
Once he caught me,
he refused to
release me,
although I
spurned his
advances.
He overpowered me,
violated me,
robbed me of
my innocence
and identity.
You'll never belong to
anyone else,
he growled in
my ear,
ignoring my pleas,
stifling my
cries for
Freedom.
You're
mine.

-Chosen

I want to be
brave,
but past
experiences with
Pain
remind me that
this
will be

difficult.

I got so
good at
pretending
that Pain wasn't
stalking me,
that it even
surprised even me
when I was
captured
again.

I don't know
why Pain
targeted me.
All I know is

no one

deserves to
suffer
like this.

Freedom and I were
childhood sweethearts,
roaming the
hills and parks
as if we were the
king and queen
of wherever
we were
together,
until the
streetlights
turned on at
sunset,
beckoning us
home.
Freedom took me
by the hand
wherever we went.
We were
the dynamic
duo
of the
schoolyard.
Freedom taught me
to live
wholly –
to laugh,
to dance,
to take
chances, and
to take up

space.
Freedom taught me
how to
love,
before I knew
there was
any other
way to
live.
Shame and
Despair
could not
tear me from
the arms
of Freedom.
The eyes of Freedom,
green as a
sunbeam
shining
through a
forest canopy,
hold no
criticism
or malice,
but rather an
invitation
to authenticity.
Freedom's voice,
soft as
dandelion seeds
floating on a summer's wind,
heals any

wound
inflicted by a
sharp word.

Before Pain
captured me from
Freedom,
I never knew
my heart could
keep beating
without him,
but I feel
no life
in my veins.
I miss
being
naive.

-Sweethearts

I am
cursed
to try to
survive Pain
and
enjoy Freedom
in the same
body.

I used to
dance with
Freedom
until Pain
cut in
and forced me
to leave.
Freedom called
after me,
but Pain
kept me from
looking back.
Freedom
threw rocks
at my window,
but Pain's searchlight
found Freedom
every time
he tried to
spring me
from my cell.
Freedom wrote me
love letters.
Pain burned them,
the ashes of
sweet promises
slipping through my
fingers.
I have been
Pain's hostage
for so long,

that I can
no longer
remember
the color of
Freedom's
eyes.

If I had known
when Pain was
coming for
me, I
never would have
let go of
Freedom's
hand.

Who am I
without Pain?
He has
stripped me of
myself.
Pain is a
narcissist,
a skilled
con man
fooling those he
hasn't stolen from.
I alone
know of
his true
cruelty
towards me,
concealing it with
years of
practice;
I needed to survive.

-Long Con

People tell me I'm a
superhero
for being able to
function despite
a life with
Pain.
What they don't
understand
is that
my body is
the villain.

Why do I
constantly
have to
fight
with myself?
Is my
body
hurting me,
or am I
hurting
my body?
I can't tell
anymore.

When Pain
comes around,
his presence
creates a
visceral
response.
Lightning strikes
through my
head,
interrupting
attempts to form
a coherent
thought.
The world
turns,
and any
meager meal
that Pain has
allowed me
is rejected.

My body
reacts to Pain
so strongly,
I question
whose side
she is
on –

his or mine?

I wish I could
regain
what Pain has
stolen
from me,
but what
Pain
has stolen
is me.

I always dreamed of
flying to
new heights to
see this
beautiful world.

But Pain has
clipped my wings
and trapped me
in a cage
made of
myself.

How am I
supposed to
find
Freedom
while Pain
keeps me
in the
darkness?

I had
hoped
I wouldn't
end up
back
here.

Silly me.

Shame and
Despair –
the pilot fish
of Pain –
give warning
that something
worse
is coming for
me,

but only
when they
feel like it.

Out the window
of my cell,
I see
people
walk by with
smiles
on their
faces.

I can tell
that Pain has
never taken
anything
from them.

-Untouched

I shake
my fist at the
sky
through the
bars
on my window,
wondering
why no one
can help.

Solitary confinement
is being
surrounded
by those that
Pain
has never robbed.

*Have you tried
opening the
window?*
Yes, that was
my first
thought.
*Have you tried
grabbing the
keys
when Pain
walks by your
cell?*
Yep, didn't
work.
Made things
worse for me,
actually.
*Have you tried
breaking through
the stone walls?*
*Have you tried
bribing the
parole officer?*
*Have you tried
not being
in prison?*
*Have you tried?
Have you tried??
Have you tried???*

Stop making

suggestions
if you have
never been held
Captive
by Pain.

-Unsolicited

I had
dreams, and
plans, and
goals.
Pain wants to
pin me down
and break
me.

Shame and
Despair
are the
opening act
and the
encore
that nobody
asked for.

Freedom came to
visit.
His hands
reached for
mine through the
bars.
Tears streamed
down my face
as I watched
him being forced
leave.

It almost makes
being stuck here
with Pain
worse, knowing
Freedom had to
leave me
behind.

Pain makes me
wear
blinders
so that all I
see
is him.

Pain loves to
play
mind games.
He wants to
break my
mind
as well as my
body.

Pain does
this thing for
fun,
where he will
ease up just
enough to
give me
false hope that
my sentence is
nearing its
end.
Then he comes in
swinging –

harder than
ever
before.

Sometimes Pain
enjoys
fanfare.
He wants me
to anticipate him
and feel
afraid.
Other times,
he attacks
without
warning,
wanting me to
feel
safe
until he pulls the
rug
out from under
me.

I know I'm
strong.
I know I'm
capable.
I know I'm
tough.
I am well
aware
of my
battle scars.
I fought
hard
to earn them.
I just wish I could
be
soft.

-Scarred

Shame
doesn't want you to
know
that Pain has
taken
other victims,
too.

It is
impossible
to sleep while
imprisoned
by Pain.
This is by
design –
Pain creates a
vicious
cycle that
weakens
your
ability to
fight.

-Insomnia

I have to
release
what I cannot
control,
but Pain
makes it feel
like I
cannot even control
myself.

-Mastermind

With all that I
have put my
body through
in order
to survive,
no wonder
she
hates me.

It is far too
quiet here.
All I can
hear
is my own
breathing.
But then the
cell block door
flings open.
Pain's pounding
footsteps
approach my cell,
each step
hitting like a
hammer
against my
head.

*How badly
does it
hurt?* they
ask.
Well,
imagine a
railroad spike
going through the
side of your
head,
but not
killing you.
Now you're a
little
closer to
understanding.

My thoughts have
become
disjointed
and the days
run
together.
How can I
fight back
if I can't even
focus?

The cost of
fighting with
Pain
is far too
great.
Pain
doesn't fight
fair.

The constant
back and
forth
with Pain
makes me feel like too
big a
burden
for Freedom to
bear.

RESIGNED

What is
supposed to be
my temple
has become
my prison.
Pain is a
thief,
and yet I
am the one
incarcerated.

If I just
resign myself to
Pain's whims,
will he go any
easier on me?

The parole
officer
shakes her
head at
me.
*I'm out of
ideas
for getting
you
out of
here,*
she confesses,
resigned.
*Why did I
bother
coming to you
for help?*
I ask,
incredulous.

I guess
I'm stuck
here.

I may be
young
in years,
but my body
betrays
what is left
of my
youth.
Pain has
taken
time off
my life.
It is
draining
me of my
already
fleeting
innocence.

How am I
supposed to
love
my body
when she
betrays me?

Pain is
a prison
I cannot
escape.
No body, no crime,
they say.
But my body
is the crime.

Pain is
a ruthless
captor –
stealing
innocence,
denying
Freedom,
and creating
enmity
between the
prisoner
and herself.

I have
nothing
left to
give,
and yet
Pain
demands
more.

Between the
bars of my
jail cell window,
I see
Freedom beckon
from the hills,
but Pain
hasn't decided
that I have served
my sentence.

When I
look at
my body,
I forget that
she was my
friend
before Pain
made us
enemies.

Pain barrels down
the hallway,
his two favorite
guards
following closely.
Inspection time!
Get your shit
together!
he bellows,
as if I
have the
strength
left to handle
such a
request.
Shame and
Despair
howl with
laughter at
the instruction.

Pain picks the
worst time
to kick you
while you are
down,
and he
invites his
friends
to watch.

Pain has
kept me
incarcerated
for so
long that
I'm beginning
to think
that this is
my
permanent
residence.

Every once
in a while,
Pain brings
me to the
prison yard
for a break
from my
cell.
I wish I could
run for the
hills
beyond the fence,
but I
know Pain will
take away my next
break if I
am anything
less than
grateful
for this
brief
respite.

Pain will
slap you
across the
face,
and then
make you
feel
guilty for
defending yourself
the next time
he raises his
hand to
strike.

-Gaslight

Pain has
transformed me
into a
shell
of who I
once was, back
when Freedom
would take me
by the
hand.
I don't
recognize
myself
when I
catch glimpses
of my
reflection.
Eyes that once
sparkled with
the light of
life
look back at me

hollow.

-Mirror

Remembering Freedom
only causes
the heartbreaking
realization
that I may

never

see him

again.

How unjust
that I am
completely
at the
mercy
of Pain and his
officers.
There is
nothing
I can do
on my own,
unless
someone else can
intervene
on my
behalf.

Dear God,

why does Pain
get to
harm
without restraint?
Why does he
get to hold me
prisoner?
I know You are
good,
but I don't
understand.
I have tried
to serve You
well.
You're supposed to
liberate the
oppressed.
I have
nothing
left to
give,
but take this
desperate cry
as my
offering.

*Why don't you just
kill me
already?!*
I scream in
Pain's face.
Pain's eyes
go black;
an ugly
sneer slowly creeps
across his
face.
*I can't
watch you
suffer if you're*

dead.

Why even bother?
Pain knows he can
lock me back up
whenever he
thirsts for
blood.

Pain has
hurt me before.
Why is he
hellbent on
destroying me this
time?

Dust and
sweat and
tears
coat my face.
Pain
provides no
comfort.

Shame and
Despair
enjoy afternoons spent
taunting me
through the cell
bars.
I'm a
circus pet
they like
to throw
trash at.

At least
in the
dark,
Pain can't
see me
cry.

-Hidden

I stopped
waking up thinking,
Today has
to be the
day,
a long time
ago.

Pain has
taught me that
some people just
want to
watch you
bleed.

I am so
tired
of being
a prisoner
to Pain,
being treated like
the sole object of his
attention.
I don't want
to be an
anomaly.

All I can
manage to do
is stare at
my cell wall
and pray
that time passes
quickly.

People look at me
like I brought
Pain upon
myself
on purpose.
Why would I
bring such
abuse
on myself?
I used to like
me.

Screaming for
help
has only made
me feel more
alone.

No one hears.
No one comes.

What does
a day without Pain
even feel like?
Have I ever
spent a day
without him
lurking
in the shadows?
I don't
remember

anymore.

*You're not worth
rescuing,*
Pain scoffs.

It takes
all of the
strength
I have left
to keep
that from
sinking in.

Living with
Pain
is a
miserable
existence.

How can I fight
Pain,
when my body
has given up
on me?

She fought a
good fight

until now.

Shame
stands outside my
cell,
twirling the
keys on his
finger,
his face
contorted in a
mocking
grin.
He was
sent by
Pain to
remind me that
I am
powerless
to their
whims.

I've been
imprisoned
by Pain
for so
long,
I don't
remember
what it
feels like to
be

normal.

Freedom once
told me that
Pain
can't hang on
forever.

I think he
underestimated
Pain's tenacity.

I can't
do this
anymore.

It's just

too

much.

Despair stares at
me through the
bars of my cell
door.
I try to
hide my
tears, but his
piercing gaze
sees through me
trying to
hide
how badly this
hurts.

-Despondent

Pain strikes me
in the head
again,
with Shame
standing
behind him.
Pain wants me to
believe
I brought this
on myself.

-Deserved

Everything that
I have walked
through before
seems so
easy now
compared to
this.

Pain has
no limits
on how
cruel
he can and
will
be.
He makes the
rules
here.

-Limitless

I have
grieved over
many things in life,
but I
never
thought
I would have
to grieve
my own death.

Sleep eludes me as
Pain sends
shockwaves
through my
body.
Unconsciousness
is my only
sanctuary.

Despair
stands outside
my cell for
hours,
repeating
over and
over, *You're
never
getting out of
here,*
until I
scream.

Pain creates a
division
between me and
my body.
I barely
know her
anymore.

Shame tries to
convince me that
Freedom
blames me
for being
trapped
here.

I wish I
were
optimistic
about the end
of this torment.
I used to be
hopeful.

Am I
wrong
for not
feeling more
hopeful?
Or am I
just being
realistic?

I wish I could
count down
the days until I am
released,
but Pain
never gave me a
proper
sentence.

RESOLVED

*Get me through
today,* I
pray weakly.
I can't
ask for much
more
than that
anymore.

*Everything
will be
okay*, I
whisper to
myself.
I try to
believe it.

*Nothing
will be okay,*
Despair
whispers back in
the dark.

A recurring
worry that I
can't seem to
shake,
and that
Shame loves to
amplify:
After
fighting so
hard...

what if
Freedom
doesn't want me
anymore?

If I'm
going to be
trapped
indefinitely
in this
prison
of my body, I
at least
wish the stone
were covered
with moss
and ivy.
Fill the
cracks
with green.
Soften the
austerity.

I vaguely
remember
what it was like
to laugh easily,
to cry happily,
to dance
when joy would
overflow me.
Oh, to be
uninhibited
by Pain
again.

I watch the
birds fly
past my cell
window and
wonder
where the
wind will
take them
next.
I used to
wonder
the same thing
about
me.
But now I am
certain
that if I
ever
get out of here,
I will
not stay
in the same
place
for long.

-Flight

I'm tired of
fighting, but I'm
more tired of
Pain getting his
way.

Exhaustion
threatens to
take control
every second of
this fight.

I can't let it
win.

I hope
Freedom
loves me
enough
for the both
of us.

I wish I
could talk to
someone who has
survived
Pain's torment.
How did they
make it
out
without
completely

collapsing?

I've lost track of
how long I've
been trapped here,
but it has been
long enough for
my tears to
water a
small flower
growing through the
crack in my
cell floor.

At least something
beautiful
happened here.

God can, and
God *will*
release me from
Pain.
I just
wish
that I didn't
have to
wait.

If we are
going to
win the
fight,
my body and
I must be
on the
same
side.

I've fought
Pain before
and won.
He refuses to
back down
this time
until I am
completely
annihilated.

-Persistent

Freedom
promised me,
*in sickness and
in health.*
I hope
he meant it.

-Vow

Dear God,

I don't know
why I'm
going through this
torment,
but I
hope
it brings me
closer
to You.

The only ways
I can
escape my
body are to
dissociate
or die.

It looks like
we will have to
find a way to
get
along.

When I finally get
released,
I can't wait to
go to the
spa, or to
hop on a plane and
go someplace
beautiful
and new, or to
go to a party.

But I also can't wait
to take a
shower, or to
grocery shop, or to
have coffee
with a
good friend.

I can't wait to
just do
normal
human things
without
Pain
dictating
my life.

The breeze through
my cell window
is like a
caress on my
cheek from
Freedom.

There are
so many things
that should have
bailed me out of
here.
I wish I didn't
have to
advocate
for myself,
but I will

if I have to.

Every second here is
time that Pain
has kept me from
Freedom's arms.

He'll pay for that.

I will
fight
like
hell
to get back to
Freedom.

There is
no other
option.

With the little
strength
I have left,
I am choosing
not to play
Pain's game
anymore.

If I have to
scream into the
void so
loudly that I
lose my
voice, in the
hope of
finally being
heard,

so be it.

Maybe if I can
outwit,
outsmart, or
outlast
Pain, I can
conquer him.

Somehow,
someday, I
must
get
out
of here.

I know
tomorrow isn't
guaranteed;
all I know
is that I
don't want to
spend it
here.

Freedom stands on the
hilltop beyond my
cell window
once again,
hand raised in a
salute.

He knows I'm
fighting
back.

Before I can
take on fighting
Pain,
I must first
defeat
Shame and
Despair.

I've done
everything I can
to prepare for
battle.
All I can
do now is
hope that I've done
enough.

Pain wants me
to bleed, but
not fight –
to scream, but
not cry.
He wants proof
that I
fear him,
and that he is
winning.
He strikes,
but I look him
in the eye
and spit in his
face.
He strikes
harder, but
I want him to
know

this time,
I won.

-Victor

My newfound
resolve
is just about the
only
weapon
I've got left.

Pain's silence doesn't
mean I am
safe,
but maybe he
needs some
recovery time now,
too.

Instead of
tally marks
decorating the
walls of my
cell,
one word is
etched
over and over:

Freedom.

I persevere
purely out of
spite.
Pain will not
have the
last word.

Pain will not
win.

If I die here,
tell Pain
that I said,
Go to hell.

-Condemn

How dare you, Pain growls, as he wipes my spit off his face. *Because* you *dared me to,* I growl back.

As long as Pain
hasn't taken the
breath from my lungs,
I will
not
stop
fighting.

In my
weakest moments,
faces flash through
my broken
mind –
loved ones,
Freedom –
and they
pick me back
up
off the
prison floor.

One way or
another, I
will find my
way
back to
Freedom.

I would love
to get back to
doing the
things I
used to
love doing
whenever I
feel like
me
again.

I can't wait to
finally
rest.
It has been
far too
long
since I have
felt any
real
peace.

Pain bursts in
swinging
hard.
I roll my
eyes at him.
*So, what else is
new?* I
mumble.
*Is that the
best you've
got?*

I will not
give him the
pleasure
of knowing
how badly it
hurts.

If Pain has
nothing else,
the one thing
he never
runs out of
is
audacity.

I'm fighting to
get back to
who I
was
before Pain
robbed me of
life.

My body is
weak,
but my
mind
is sharper
than ever
since I resolved to
fight back.

For all the
scars that
Pain has
inflicted on
me,
I hope I
can give
him a few
back.

It takes
everything you have
to
stand up to
Pain,
and it is
still
not
enough.

I absolutely
hate
that
I cannot
escape
or be
bailed out of
here.
Pain gets the
satisfaction
of being
responsible for my
release.

He doesn't
deserve
that.

-Unworthy

As much as I
want to
fight, I
can't shake the
truth.
Eventually,
Pain will
throw me in here

again.

RELEASED

When I get
out of here,
I refuse
to be held
back
from living.

Pain saunters up
to my cell door,
keys in hand.
*You've earned
your
parole,*
he sneers.
*Enjoy it
while it lasts.*

I call, and
Freedom
answers,
I can't wait to see you.
Trembling, I
confess,
*Pain did a
number on me.
I'm not the
same as I was
before.*
Freedom
reminds me,
*But you're
still
you.*

Pain won't tell me
how long I am
granted
parole.
He could
throw me back in
at any
moment.
I wish I could
live life
without
constantly
looking over
my shoulder.

My body and
I have to
reconcile –
we've been at
war
for too
long.

Freedom waits
on the
other side of my
cell door.
Pain
unlocks the door
with
Shame and
Despair
standing behind him.
As I leave my
cell, I
defiantly
raise my chin,
pull back my
shoulders, and
stare
each of them
in the
eye.
I turn,
and don't
look
back.

Freedom holds my
hand in the
car as we drive
away
from the
prison.
Out of
fear of Pain's
sick games returning,
I refuse to
tell myself
that I am going
home
until we
get there.

*It's been so
long
since I've
danced,*
I say to
Freedom, *I'm
not sure I
remember
how.*
Freedom takes me
gently by
the hand.
*I'll
show you.*

Rain is
pouring down
when Freedom
brings me
home.
It is like
God is
telling us it's
time to
dance again.

-Rain Dance

I step into our
home
for the first
time since
Pain
captured me.
I have to
find my
bearings again.
Everything feels
familiar yet
foreign.

The first morning
at home –
waking up to the
sun shining through my
barless window
and Freedom by my
side –
reminds me that
peace is
real
and it is now
ours.

The world is
so much
bigger
now that I've been
liberated.

I will not
to take the days
without Pain
for granted
ever
again.

I am trying to
make the
most of the
time I have
away from
prison.
It is
hard to
forget the
reality that
Pain will
return for me

anytime
he feels like it.

It has been so
long
since I have felt
joy, or
romance, or
spontaneity.
I need to
learn
how to
feel
again.

People ask me
how I've
been
after not
seeing me for so
long.
They don't
remember
that I was in
Pain's prison
again.
*I've been
okay*, I
lie.

Everything that I
have gone
through
hits me in
waves.
I have to
let myself
experience both
profound joy
and
deep grief
simultaneously.

My sentence
has ended,
yet the
dark circles
still surround my
eyes.
My body
can't remember
life beyond
the cell.

*You're so
strong*, they
say after
learning of my
battles with
Pain.

I wish I
didn't
have to
be.

I am trying to
make myself at
home in my
body again,
but she
hasn't
always been a
safe space.

I just have to
keep going
as if I were
never
incarcerated.
Even if I can't,
life keeps
moving on with
or without me.

The world kept
turning
while I was in my cell.
I've missed
so much,
but have no
idea
how to
catch up.

Freedom sees the
fear in my
eyes
when I spot Pain
lurking in the
shadows.
He takes me in
his arms,
knowing
that I will
likely be
Pain's hostage
once again.

-Protect

It cost me
too much
to get to this
point.
I wish parole could
last
longer.

If only I
could find a
way to
stop Pain
before he
attacks.

-Preventative

How do you manage with Pain so well? people ask me.

I don't.
I'm just good at making you think
I do.

-Trick

If I tell you
that I've
been
*hanging in
there,*
I actually
mean that I'm
hanging on by a
thread.

*I don't know
how you
do it,* they
say, trying to be
encouraging.
What they
don't
understand
is that I
have no
other
options.

I must approach
each day of
parole
one at a
time
to truly
feel it.

Having the ability to
say yes
or no
to anything –
to choose how I
spend my days
without restriction
or punishment –
is a privilege for which I
will always be
grateful.

I can't be
naive
and pretend that
Pain won't
come for me
again.
But I can
take advantage
of every
second I have
until his
return.

I never want to
take Freedom
for granted.
Every moment
of our reunion
is a
precious
gift.

If I only have
today
before Pain
returns for me,
take me
somewhere
green,
where we can
can get
lost in the
trees.

Anytime I see
another person
with familiar
scars
and tired
eyes,
I know that
Pain
has tortured them,
too.

Those who
have been
robbed by Pain
understand
that life can be
both
beautiful and
horrific,
often at the
same
time.

I don't need to have
all the answers.

I just need to

be.

It's time to
burn the
disguises
and masks
I have used to
conceal the
scars that
Pain gave me.
Hiding them only
allows him to
continue without
repercussions.

Freedom
reminds me that
I am
worthy of
joy
regardless of
the lies that
Pain spreads.

I am not what
Pain has done
to me.
I am not my
scars.
I am not my
trauma.
I am more
than what I have
been through.
I am

me.

I wish I could have warned
my younger self
what was coming.
But –
I wouldn't want to
rob her of the
joy and
innocence
of life
without Pain.

It is so
wonderful
to
sleep in
peace
again.

The only part
Pain will get to
play
in my
story
is the villain
that I
eventually
defeat.

If we
report Pain's
many crimes,
maybe we can
incarcerate him
for life.

I am more
than the
scars I have
accumulated
from Pain.

Although, I
hope they
expose him
as the
monster
he is.

Pain won't get
any credit
for giving me
a story to
tell.
He will only
get credit
as my
abuser.

There will come a
day when
Pain is finally
vanquished
from this world.

I hope I'm there to
see him get
what he
deserves.

-Justice

Life is a
pile of
good and
bad days.
As awful and
unwanted
as the bad days
are, the
good days that
follow sure seem

sweeter.

Freedom runs
up to me,
luggage in
hand.
Let's go, he
says, grinning.
I can't
wait
to see where
he takes me
next.

*Let's run
away
like
vagabonds,*
I say, taking
Freedom by the
hand.
*Take me
somewhere
Pain can't
find me.*

If we're all
just stories
in the end,
I hope that
mine
is one of
perseverance.

Pain will
strike
again.
But I will
win

again.

-Ready

ACKNOWLEDGMENTS

THANK YOU

This book would not have come to life without the help of my amazing friends and family. Thank you for always believing in me and encouraging me. I love you so much.

Lex - my sweet, wonderful husband – I could not have finished this project without your endless love and support. Thank you for being my biggest fan and my very best friend. Thank you so much for designing the most beautiful book cover, and for putting up with me bolting upright in the middle of the night to scribble down lines in my journal in the dark, praying that they'll be legible in the morning.

Nikki – thank you for walking me through the whole process of self-publishing, and for cheering me on through it. I am so thankful to have you as a hype woman and as a beloved friend. *(And the rest of you – go check out her work on Instagram @nixwrites_)*

Melanie, Stephanie, Emma, and Kim – thank you for being such wonderful and supportive ARC readers. Melissa – thank you for being the most incredible proofreader and copyeditor. All of your feedback and encouragement have been tremendously helpful.

And you! Dear reader, thank you so much for picking up a copy of this book. I hope that it has made you feel seen, or that it has challenged you in some way. Sharing these words and my heart with you means the world and more to me.

ABOUT THE AUTHOR

Lindsay Gordon is a youth pastor, singer, dog mom, and cancer survivor. After growing up in Chicagoland with a love of reading and writing, she received her degree in English Education from Olivet Nazarene University. When she is not writing, you can find her in the forest or the mountains with her husband, Lex, and her dog, Rocket. As an extrovert, Lindsay loves connecting with different people. You can find her and her upcoming work on Instagram @linesbylinds, or at linesbylinds.com.

Printed in the USA
CPSIA information can be obtained
at www.ICGtesting.com
LVHW020126130424
777223LV00012B/275